The Shapes of Things

Michael Swan

Oversteps Books

First published in 2011 by

Oversteps Books Ltd
6 Halwell House
South Pool
Nr Kingsbridge
Devon
TQ7 2RX
UK

www.overstepsbooks.com

Copyright © 2011 Michael Swan
ISBN 978-1-906856-19-9

Printed in Great Britain by imprint digital, Devon.

for Catherine

Acknowledgements

Poems in this collection have been previously published in
Acumen, Envoi, Frogmore Papers, Orbis, Poetry News,
Poetry Nottingham, Seam, Smiths Knoll, The New Writer,
The Rialto, The Spectator,
and in anthologies of prize-winning and commended entries
for the Arvon, Poetry on the Lake, Stephen Spender and
Torbay competitions.

Contents

The Shapes of Things

A circle for his mother's face;
circles for apples, oranges, the sun.

Squares and triangles
with his birthday crayons
for their tiny house;
a wavy line for the chimney-smoke.

It was always the shapes of things.

What a gift
with nothing but brushes and paint
to find the shape of a hawk circling,
a duststorm,
a woman's head turning.

Nobody understood
how he could fit them
into such a small space:
the shape of loving,
the shapes of hurt and comfort,
joy and despair.

He learnt the shape of fast cornering,
of seduction,
of smart parties in the best circles,
of power and respect.
He found out the special shape of money.

Do you know the shape of illness,
of unpaid bills,
of friends who let you down?
The shape of loss?
Look at his self-portraits.

Look at those eyes
that learnt the shape of the whole world.

On the last day of his life
leaning on a stick, trembling in front of the easel
he drew a perfect circle.

How Everything Is

Perhaps this is how everything is.
The scree steepens into rockface;
you work your way up ten or twelve pitches,
each worse than the one before,
the last a brutal overhang
with few holds, and those not good;
somehow, pushing your limits,
you struggle through to the top
with your arms on fire,
to find a car park, toilets and a café.

Tiger Dreams

Child
one day
you will meet a tiger.

You and the tiger
face to face.

What will you do?

I know you.
You will hold out
to the tiger
on your bare hand
a small globe
spinning,
throwing light at all angles.
And you will tell the tiger your dreams,
and a special thing
that only you know.

And the tiger will come close,
press her muzzle to you
 – if she were not a wild creature
you would swear
it was a kiss.
And in her turn
she will tell you a secret.

For a long time
you will share each other's eyes.

You will go away
pad, pad, pad;
and when no one is looking
you will wash your fur
with your rough tongue.

And the tiger
will tell your dreams
to her babies.

Comb

I was sure
it was her comb
lying on the pavement.
And I ran after her
shouting
'Excuse me
but you dropped your comb'
and she turned
a woman I had never seen before
and she told me
no
it was not her comb.
She seemed unwilling
to discuss the matter further
and walked on
rather quickly.
She had hair like yours
and the comb, too,
was like one of those
you used to leave everywhere
on tables, shelves, windowledges,
in the car, on your pillow.

I was sure it was your comb.

Happy Ending

They don't die
after the balcony,
the night of love,
such sweet sorrow
and the rest.

On the contrary,
they save up for a deposit,
and she gets a job
at Marks and Spencer's
till the first kid comes along.

He gets promoted to area manager,
and then head of marketing.

Tennis at the weekend.
Costa Brava or Scotland in the summer.
One year, the Seychelles.

A good retirement package.
They move to Dunstable.

They see the grandchildren quite often.
She knits things for them.
He teaches them tricks,
and wiggles his ears
to make them laugh.

Not such a good story?
Ask him. Ask her.

Not what I Meant

Food and water were plentiful.

I had a little house
made from the boat's timbers.

I got up every day
before dawn
because of the spiders' webs.

Have you seen spiders' webs
with the dew on them
in the early sun?

And in the evening
did you know
the colours on the clouds
are exactly reflected
in the surf?

And the moon, then,
makes a line of gold
from the beach to the horizon.

I knew all the birds,
the small animals
and the trees.

And there were porpoises.

The only sadness:
such beauty
and no one to share.

One day, a ship.
I jumped up and down
on the big rock.
I waved my flag –
a shirt on a stick.

'Come and look!'
I shouted.
'The spiders' webs
the shells
the blossom
the birds of paradise
the moon!'

They took me away
and gave me potatoes and beef.

I said 'No.
No,
No.'

They gave me new clothes
and cut my hair.

I said
'That was not what I meant.'

I told the TV people
about the porpoises
and the shells and the blossom.

I told the doctors
about the spiders' webs
and the line of the moon.

I said
'Yes, I waved my flag
but that was not what I meant.

That was not what I meant.'

Marco Polo

I was talking to Marco Polo.

He said
Yes, OK,
he went over the top a bit
in the book
to push up the sales.

But it was mostly true.

The years on the road.
Turkey, Armenia, Persia, Afghanistan, ...

Disease,
and a year to recuperate
in Badakhshan.

Bandits,
sandstorms and spirit voices
in the Gobi.

The Pamirs were the worst
he said,
with the bloody horses dying
below the high passes
where your bones froze.

You know
I said
I was in China yesterday.
(True enough.
We hit Terminal 3
at 7.20 this morning.)

I had expected disbelief,
but he understood pretty well
what we can do.

I had not expected pity.

'It's not quite that,' said the Grandmaster

'I live in terror,'
said the Grandmaster.

'I know just what you mean,'
I said.
'Life at the top:
one day, world-famous,
next day, nobody.'

'It's not quite that,'
said the Grandmaster.
'It's more the travelling.'

'Yes, indeed,' I said.
'I understand completely.
The ever-present fear of an accident.
In your mind's eye
you see all too vividly
your shattered body
lifeless on a Siberian hillside
surrounded by the fragments
of your ivory chess set.'

'It's not quite that,'
said the Grandmaster.
'It's more the thought
that one day
next to me on the plane
there will be a woman
whose eyes, whose perfume,
and other things
will cause me to lose my senses.
Evading the reception committee
I will go with her to her far-off home,
where she will drain me to a husk
and discard me.
Her brothers will drive me out into the forest
and I will be pursued by wolves.'

'I see it all,' I said.

'Your flesh torn by those savage jaws,
your blood seeping into the forest floor.'

'It's not quite that,'
said the Grandmaster ...

One of a Series

'My word,'
I said,
'That really is
a remarkable likeness
of a cold fried egg
on a chipped plate.
How much is it?'

'Actually,'
they said.
'It *is* a cold fried egg
on a chipped plate.
It is one of a series
created
by Laura Carambo.

£150,000.'

And I said
'?????'

And they said
'This is not just
any cold fried egg
on any chipped plate.
It is *this* cold fried egg
on *this* chipped plate.

Carambo's work celebrates
the *thisness* of things.

She shows us how
this and *the other*
move in a perpetual dance,
mediating between
and uniting
the amphimetropic opposites
of our Janus-faced universe.'

Well
I could see that it all made sense.
And between you and me,
I've looked at the reviews
and the auction catalogues,
and I reckon
I got a real bargain.
Come and look.

Armadillo

I didn't like to ask
about the armadillo.
Maybe Julia had brought it,
and she does not always welcome questions.

I could just imagine it:
'Why have I brought an armadillo
into the house?
Well, why shouldn't I?
What have you got against armadillos?
You're always trying to control me.
I never said anything
when you parked your motorbike in the hall
for months on end.
And that reminds me.
When your mother was here ...'

So you will understand
why I chose not to go down that road,
but just gave the creature some milk
and made it a bed by the fridge.

It settled down
and was perhaps on the way to becoming
a valued member of the household
when Julia came in, and said
'What the hell
is that bloody animal
doing in the house?
You're always bringing things in
without asking me.
There was that blasted motorbike
that you parked in the hall
for months on end.
And that reminds me.
When your mother was here ...'

Emails

With emails
everything is transformed.

Years ago
you put a stamp on your heart
posted it
and waited days
for the reply.

Not so now.

Yesterday I wrote
telling her I missed her.
My life is empty
with you away
I said,
a mockery.
I go through the motions
but all is dead.

Not ten minutes
and her answer
had winged its way back.

Don't forget to pay Mrs Blake,
she said.
I think we need more catfood,
and if Oliver rings
tell him the minutes are on their way.

It's Wednesday

If you want to understand them,
you have to start with their language,
which is different from ours.
For example, when we say 'It's Wednesday',
'it's' means 'it's'
and 'Wednesday' means 'Wednesday'.
When they say 'It's Wednesday'
they mean 'Put the bins out'
or 'Remember Granny's coming to supper'
or 'Jessica's got her maths exam'
or 'It's your turn to babysit'
or 'Why haven't you –––?' (fill in the blank)
or 'You bastard, you've forgotten our anniversary'
or just 'Guess what's in my head'.
There are no dictionaries.
Good luck.

Spare a Thought

Spare a thought
for the old wise man
sitting on a mountain
cross-legged
with leaves in his beard.

He has fleas,
and he really smells quite awful,
worse than a bear.
The animals skirt around him.

But from his perch
his eyes range deep into space;
they bring back understanding
from across the galaxies.

Decades of meditation
have given him
insights more precious
than iron
the potter's wheel
the alphabet or gunpowder.

He alone knows
what is to come.

And all that is needed
is that one person
– man, woman, child, no matter –
climb the overgrown trail.

But the chances are not good.

Spare a thought
for the old wise man
with leaves in his beard.

The Fisherman's Daughter

The fisherman's daughter
is visiting her cousin
in the mountains.
It is cold,
the roofs are the wrong shape,
and the faces are closed.
She misses the sound of the sea.

But the peaks
that change places with the clouds
tell her things
that she strains to hear,
and the music
from the square in the evening
speaks a language
that she knew before she was born.

In front of the mirror
in the hayloft
where they have made her a bed,
she brushes her long black hair,
shivers,
and thinks of her lover.

From the Ancient Germanic

Do not talk to the gods.
They are a rowdy lot
and can turn nasty.
You should avoid
attracting their attention.

Do not talk to the clouds.
They will consider it
an impertinence.

Do not talk to the rocks.
They are the custodians of time.
Your words
will mean nothing to them.

Do not talk to yourself.
You will learn little
and the children
will throw stones at you.

Talk to people
if you wish,
but be warned
that complications will ensue.

Myself
I would advise
the trees and the plants.

Not the great elm
the towering beech
the ancient oak,
or the pines and firs
of the dark forests.

Talk, rather
to the graceful birch
the gentle willow
the wise quiet ash.
Talk to the cowslip
and the saxifrage.

They will welcome your confidences.

Above the Snow

Touring my estate
after the funeral
I leave no footprints
in the snow.

'Look, Highness,'
they say,
'Here, your royal heels
left their mark,
and here, and here.'

Can they not see
it is a trick of the light?

I wear silk,
and I do not move the air
that I move through.
My sheets
in the morning
bear no impress.
I disturb, displace nothing.

I stay always
a little above the snow
as befits my station.

They bow
and carry out my orders
and laugh behind their hands
and understand nothing.

Grief
for a dead woman?
Why would I feel grief?

I leave no footprints.

A Small Snowdrift

I passed a small snowdrift
on my way to the station,
there on the corner
just outside Buckingham's.
It was in quite good shape,
though a little dirty
and looking furtive
as well it might
on a hot day in August
and no snow since March.
Just one more of us,
it was all too clear,
in the right place
at the wrong time,
or the wrong place
at the right time.
So I threw the creature
a comradely glance
and a quick word
to wish it good fortune,
before going on
about the day's business.

Once in a blue moon

you go to check a word
and the dictionary falls open
just at the right page.

Entranced by the gift
you read everything:
once to onion,
blue to blunder,
moon to morganite
– such riches.

And sometimes it happens
outside the book:
hallo to happy,
idea to idyll,
love to luminosity.

Once in a blue moon.

A Legend of the Flood

I ran off with a sea-king's daughter,
brought her back to my high country,
and found us a home, deep in a combe,
walled with heather, bedded with bracken.
No view of the sea.

We had two children: a girl and a boy,
with long thin bones and grey-green eyes.
She made them a garden with samphire, sea-holly,
and salt-marsh plants which did not thrive.
No more did she.

I planted her grave with flowers from the salt marsh,
with samphire and sea-holly. They grew well.
Gulls flew over the place, crying.
I fancied her spirit was flying with them,
alive and free.

For forty days and nights it has rained
till not a roof can be seen, not a spire.
And now I stand on the highest rock.
Weed floats on the water like her hair,
and I wait for the sea.

From the Diary of Olwen Rasmussen, May 1864

Dark outside, inside.
How can we hold it at bay,
keep our little clearing open?

It presses in so.
You cannot see two hundred yards.
We ache, ache, from pushing back.

At night, the animals scream.
Why does God want so much hurt?
But He is not here.
I would not tell Lars, but God is not here.

Lars is not the same man.
He is good to me,
but the boy who laughed is dead,
gone into the dark.

He says they will not attack.
He strides out
fearless under the dark trees,
while the sun rises, and turns in the sky, and sets,
and I stand and prepare food.

It seems
in their language
they have no word for kindness.

I miss small things:
flowers in the hedges, milestones,
good butter, bacon,
a clear sky over the mountain.

I fear for the boys.
I have taught them their letters,
but there is no school since Ole died,
and where would we find books?
So they hunt with the men,
and every day their sweet faces
are harder, darker.

To be brave now, Anna says,
is incumbent on all of us.

I will be brave now,
push back,
sing into the dark.

Lance-Corporal Swan

Boys' Brigade
All London Challenge Cup 1923.
On the left a young stranger, my father,
Lance-Corporal Swan,
18 years old,
pill-box hat, cross-belt,
smart as a sunrise.

The photo over,
they swap punches,
have a smoke,
chat a bit,
head off home.

Out of the gate
he turns right
and walks whistling
down a winding road.
Behind a tree
amputation stands waiting;
round the corner
my mother moves into ambush;
at the second bend,
doctors aim their stethoscopes;
up the hill
madness crouches in the bushes,
swinging his great cudgel.

Painting a Bird

He thought
the way to do it was
to look very carefully at the bird,
so the picture was the bird itself.
But at the last moment
the bird always flew away.

Perhaps if he killed the bird
he thought,
nailed it down ...
He spent a fortune on nails
but the picture
never flew away.

Or if he fell in love with the bird:
himself and the bird
one.
But to fall in love with a bird!
There are practical problems.
It didn't go well.

To *become* a bird, then.
He put on a suit of feathers;
took lessons
from a celebrated mime.

But
as you and I could have told him
it is not a matter of imitation.
It is a journey
inwards.

He went inwards.
He went deep.
He found the bird within
and embraced it
with his whole being.

And he painted a picture
so perfect
you could almost see it breathing
trembling on the branch
ready to soar.

In the trees, meanwhile,
the birds went about their business.

The Wolf-man

When they brought him
we could see he would do no harm,
though the dogs were not easy with him.

Our doors were always open.
He could go in and out,
sleep where he liked.

Sometimes he would stay for days,
help around the house,
play with the children.
He liked to watch TV
but would not look at crying or shooting.

Then later
he would greet us like strangers
and disappear,
scuttling down a side street,
leaping a neighbour's fence.

Everybody said
his eyes were very beautiful.

He learnt our language well,
especially the beginnings of words,
which are generally easier.

With his allowance
he bought shoes.

Scientists came constantly,
measured him,
attached wires
with small pieces of plaster.
They asked him questions
but seemed disappointed with the answers,
though he told them
how to bring down a buffalo
and where to find water in the dry season.

One day he took a bus
south, to the edge of the jungle;
went sniffing along the trails
in his shiny new shoes.

Local Currency

In hell there is a bar
where you can buy cooling drinks.

You can pay
in local currency.

There are three ways
to get currency in hell.

You can make the devil cry.
A fortune for each tear
if you can get it.

Or you can perform
an act of pure love.
This has never been done.

Or you can sell time –
add years to your sentence.

As your sentence is eternity
that should make no difference.
But the view in hell
is that one cannot be sure of this.

Hope dies hard in hell.

A Request to the Archaeologists

Come to the place quietly.
Leave your vehicles out of sight.

This is what there is.
Woods, river and hills,
dust, sun and spring rain.

It was ours.

Take your smallest tools;
dig slowly.
When you come to our bones,
use tiny brushes,
let the wind help you.

Leave our little bracelets
where they are.

Look carefully
as you uncover us.
Imagine, if you can,
the flesh back onto our skulls.
Listen
as our lips whisper a greeting.

Why did we build our houses in a circle?
But every child knows the reason.
Because the sky is a circle.
Because all life returns to its beginning.
Because you must make a wall
to keep out the wolves.

The walls are down now,
and the wolves are in.

When you drive home,
finish your reports,
and sit out in the evening,
think: this is what there is.
Woods, river and hills,
the wind, and a light rain, clearing;
children in the next yard.

And remember us.

Journey of the Magi

The desert put us all in our places.

By night
ten thousand frozen stars ignored us.

By day
the sun kept its own counsel
indifferent rocks cracked in the heat
mirages danced for themselves alone.

As we walked
wind from the beginning of time
wiped out our footprints.

At dusk, yesterday
a sand-cat killed and ate a viper
two yards from me, as if I was nothing.

And this baby, Lord of Humankind?
Kings don't count for much here.

Bridge

Such a short little bridge
and you in the middle.

One step forward,
and you are on the mountain
with the heather
the clear streams
the cry of the curlew,
and no way back.

One step back,
and you are in the meadow
with the gentle animals
the young trees
the sweet grass,
and the gate closed.

And you stand there.

Night comes
and the next day
and the day after,
and still you stand there,
till the black crows arrive.

Vivaldi's Burial

All his life
he saw the numbers in things,
teased out their harmonies,
turned the whole world
to most rigorous music.

He watched the dust swirling
over the fields of the Veneto,
wrote down its patterns,
scored them for trumpet and flute.

He measured the scent of flowers,
wrote the multiplication tables of the clouds,
enumerated the wind,
drew the graph of the sun through the seasons,
fixed precisely the algebra of birdsong,
gave each its instrument,
set them gloriously together.

One of his orphans
said 'Father Antonio,
your music must give so much pleasure to God.'

He wondered sometimes
if God knew what he knew.

In his seventies
out of fashion
he went to Vienna,
had no luck,
died after nine days.

As they lowered him into a pauper's grave,
an old priest, once famous,
his last equation cancelled out,
there was no one to play.

Only
the sun shone,
the scent of flowers drifted in the wind,
clouds passed,
birds sang;
dust swirled over his grave.

Sometimes

The trouble is, it goes too fast to catch.
So many things begin. So many end.
People are kind, then not. You save, you spend.
Hares run and dance; you haven't time to watch.
Somewhere a woman sits and cries in church.
A big boy steals his little brother's toys.
Creation sings its song – you hate the noise.
Catkins are sudden on the silver birch.

Sometimes you really think you understand.
Just for a moment, high above the trees
the moon on snow is everything there is.
And then it slips out of your clumsy hands.
The moon, the hares, the catkins and the rest, all
straws in a gale.

The Twelfth Labour

Cerberus stood there snarling, acting tough,
a real performance. When he tried to fight
I blew down all six ears to call his bluff,
brought him to heel, and headed for the light.
You should have seen his faces, at the sight
of sunshine, flowers and rabbits. He went mad,
charged round all day, slept on my bed all night.
I had a friend: the first I'd ever had.
He could not settle, though, with us above.
He pined for darkness. And I was afraid,
for when the fit comes, I kill those I love,
as the gods know. A twelfth time, then, I paid:
I took him to the trail that leads below,
kissed his three muzzles, wept, and let him go.

Playing Along

All of us
putting our feet down
so carefully.

Because of the glass globes –
thin spun glass,
all colours –
that have drifted in
on the wind.

And we hear
there will be more.

Someone
is playing with us.
Someone
is laughing and laughing
at us.

And we, fools,
playing along.

All of us
putting our feet down
so carefully.

Shoulders

Each of you
she said
has a guardian angel
on one shoulder
and on the other
a devil.
You must listen to the angel
and do good things,
not the devil
and do bad things.

I was glad to have guidelines
because what with the bombs
and Daddy
it was all a bit complicated.

The trouble was
which was which.
I had 'L'
on my left hand
and 'R' on my right
in indelible pencil,
so I asked her to put
'A' on one shoulder,
and 'D' on the other,
but she smacked me.

It got no better
over the years.

I wasn't there

I wasn't there.
It was certainly someone else
who looked like me.

The women crying –
I had nothing to do with that.

You mention a child
plagued by sad memories.
I repeat
I was not there.

Photographic evidence
is not admissible.

People took so much trouble
and all their efforts
went for nothing?
I am sorry
but at the time
I was in Interlaken
or possibly Reykjavik
engaged on another matter.

My signature
on the documents
is a forgery.

Disappointment,
a sense of being let down,
of not being loved,
of being lied to?

Yes,
such feelings
are indeed distressing
and my sympathy goes out
to those concerned.

My diaries
for that period
show clearly
that I was elsewhere.

A Word

A word comes out
pulls another after it
and another
until there is a whole line of words
jostling
like women in wartime
queuing at a shop
where they have heard
there will be bread;
but it is only a rumour,
there is no bread,
and the words disperse
and go their separate ways.

A word comes out
inspects the assembled company
and goes back in.

A word comes out
catches fire
and explodes.
Sparks sear the sky
the forest flames
into a firestorm
rocks glow red
crack in the heat.

The smoke dies down
and we look at one another
across the ashes.

They say there are seeds
that will only germinate
after a fire.

I pray
that this may be so.

From a Book

That child,
they said,
always has his head buried
in a book.

True enough.
I learnt many things from books.

Rock-climbing, for instance,
though the rocks,
it became clear later,
had not read the same book.

Similar issues arose
in the swimming-pool
and on the dance floor.

Love was a particular problem.
The text
was in an unknown language,
though the book
had many attractive illustrations.

And life.
Quite useless, this one,
and the last page missing.

Not in so many Words

I remember them saying
When we lived in Britannia Row …
When we lived in Morden …
When we lived in Kelross Road …
When we lived in Swiss Cottage …

I don't remember them saying
When we were first together …
When everything seemed possible …
When we were full of life and hope …
When we loved each other …

Not in so many words.

Sense-of-Humour Failure

God played a joke
on my poor father:
took away an arm.

How they roared,
gawping
through the glass floor of Heaven
at the old boy
flailing about.

In time, though,
he learnt to manage
pretty well;
could even tie his shoes
with one hand.

So God, never at a loss,
thought up another fine wheeze:
a kidney;
and followed this up
with a lung.

They howled.
They slapped their holy thighs.
They rolled around on the clouds.
Even the Archangels
sniggered a bit
behind their wings.

Excited by the success
of his three-pronged jape,
God then
added madness.

My poor father died,
too young,
in a room with green walls,
of sense-of-humour failure.

Outside

Good, sometimes
to go outside
and walk round yourself
looking in the windows.

There are lights blazing
in rooms you have never seen;
strangers dancing,
reading,
quarrelling;
things going on
you can scarcely credit.

Only
don't stay out too long.
They might change the locks.

On the Plus Side

I've forgotten the answer.

Would you believe it?
All those years
tirelessly travelling
searching the archives
consulting authorities
tracking down eyewitnesses
collating the evidence –
all gone for nothing.
I've forgotten the answer.

On the plus side
I've forgotten the question.

Opera
after Ogden Nash

While some entertainments are not considered proper, others
      are deemed much properer,
And the properest of all is undoubtedly opera.
But I can never remember whether we are seeing La Traviata
      or Il Trovatore,
And whatever it is, I cannot make any sense of the story.
Because in opera they all dress up as each other,
So the Count ends up confusing his girl-friend with his mother
Despite the fact that the latter is much larger than the former,
      and sings bass,
But she is holding a piece of cardboard with two eyeholes
      in front of her face,
And in the world of opera this counts as an adequate disguise.
Also, there is the fact that everybody sings very healthily for a
      long time when he or she dies.
And furthermore, when you get two young lovers like Tristan
      and Isolde,
They are both forty pounds heavier than you expect, and fifty
      years older.
So please do not attempt to take me to Figaro or Lucia di
      Lammermoor:
I would relish sitting in a swamp being hit on the head with a
      hammer more.
I hope you enjoy your evening at La Bohème or the Magic
      Flute or Carmen.
Speaking for myself, I plan to renew acquaintance with
      several barmen.

Parrot

The parrot is in the forest.
The parrot is green and gold.
The parrot is having a great old time
flashing about in the treetops.

The poem is about the parrot.
The poem is black and white.
The poem is full of words.
It is not very easy to understand.

The lecture is about the poem.
The lecture is extremely full of words.
The lecture is excessively tedious.
In the front row
several grey nuns are taking notes.

The parrot did well not to come.

700

This is my seven-hundredth poem.

I have done my best for it
but with all those mouths to feed ...

Rhymes are out of the question,
let alone
anything more up-to-date.

Accompanied by its faithful cat
it sets off for London
to seek its fortune.

Gold, it soon finds out,
is not what the streets are paved with.

It keeps body and soul together
with a bit of busking
and hangs about at readings
trying to ape its betters.

One day
in a bookshop
it gets talking to a rich woman
who likes cats.

For a spell
it rides about
in her magazine.
It is accepted in literary circles
and quoted everywhere.

Then,
tiring of its rustic simplicity,
she kicks it out.
The cat, too.

Sic transit gloria mundi.
And indeed
right through the week.

It ends up in a skip
in Leicester Square
clutching the cat for warmth
and wishing it had never been written.

I feel awful.

Take it or Leave it

This poem showed up
the other day
and asked me to write it.

OK
I said
state your requirements.

Well, it said
I was thinking
maybe a sonnet
with some slick rhymes
a pervasive note of melancholy
and a neat twist at the end.

I don't do sonnets
I said,
and rhymes are right out.
I could knock you up
a nice ten-liner on sunsets.

I don't like sunsets
it said.

Well
it's sunsets or autumn leaves
I said.
Take it or leave it.

Yeah, right
it said.
I'll let you know.

If this were a Bus

If this were a bus
things would be easier.

Imagine
a stop at a dusty corner
with a jacaranda.
A woman gets on
holding two chickens.
She greets everybody
sits down
and closes her eyes.

You jolt on to the next stop,
by the garage.
An old man gets off.
He says something to the driver
that you don't catch
and aren't meant to.
Three children climb on
pinching each other,
and also a woman
who is worth a couple of looks, and more.

On to the next stop
just after the bridge,
and the next, at the crossroads,
and the next.
People get on and off,
on and off,
only, as the sun gets lower,
more off than on,
and you're alone suddenly.

The bus doesn't stop any more.
The driver is grinning at you
in the mirror.

He knows where you're going,
that's for sure,
but you don't like to say
'Look, I don't understand anything.
I don't know what's going on'.

But I tell you
it would still be easier.
if this were a bus.

A Humble Request

All right
I understand
I can't come in.

My life was –
I know.

But
if I could just
sit outside the gates
for a few minutes
and listen to the music?

We, It

We build cathedrals.
It builds mountains.

It is in trees, in the air, under the ground.
We are where we stand.

We make songs and symphonies.
It makes all the sounds of the rain.

It shapes sand and ice.
We carve statues of gods,

and construct empires and destinies.
But we cannot make a flower or an ant.

It is what it is.
We are what we are.

As we walk, dance, run,
it moves with the moon.

It has no dreams,
or any concern with us.

We think and talk.
It drops snow on the hawthorn, so gently.

It does not love or hate,
or laugh with us, or cry.

We pass on.
It remains.

God, my Good Neighbour

Translation of 'Du Nachbar Gott' by Rainer Maria Rilke

God, my good neighbour, if you sometimes hear
me knocking in the dead of night, I'm sorry.
I can't tell if you're breathing, and I worry:
I know you're all alone in there.
There's nobody to watch, or understand
if you need something – say, a glass of wine.
I listen day and night. Give me a sign.
I'm near at hand.

Chance, nothing more, has set this flimsy wall
between us. And who knows, perhaps
if you or I could bring ourselves to call,
it might collapse
quietly, and leave no trace.

The wall is built of pictures of your face.

Your pictures stand in front of you like names.
And if for once my inner light shines through
and blazes up, so that it might show who
and what you are, it's scattered by their frames.

And all my senses die back with the flames,
and are left homeless, and cut off from you.

Not Quite

The poem is never quite
what you wanted to say.

Even the great one,
the ultimate masterpiece –
ten lines only, but
all other writers
throw down their pens in despair;
in a matter of weeks
the whole world
has it by heart;
it is quoted at meetings and partings,
at weddings and funerals;
so profound is its message
that wars are stopped in their tracks;
an authority
wise and benign
is set up in Andorra la Vella
to govern the planet;
on the walls of the parliament building
in letters of gold
your text is inscribed –

even so,
it's not quite
what you wanted to say.

Other books published by Oversteps